To my mother, Madhuchhanda.

Thank you for believing in me and always having my back.

• • •

CELEBRITY PERSONALITY INDICIA PROTECTION FOR "VOICE" AND LIKELINESS

A COMPARATIVE LEGAL ANALYSIS BETWEEN U.S., U.K., AUSTRALIA AND INDIA

SAATHI MUKHERJEE

Contents

Preface

The purpose of this book is to bring into light the significance and importance of *"voice"* in regard to a celebrity's identity. It adds onto his/her persona. Therefore, *"voice"* must be protected. It has been discussed using various legislations, Intellectual Property Regime and Tort Law in various jurisdictions like the United States, the United Kingdom, Australia and India. Further, by the method of elimination it has been determined how *"voice"* cannot be protected within the ambit of the mentioned legislations. Later on it has been argued using valid case laws and arguments how publicity rights is the solution to this as *"voice"* is just as distinctive as a celebrity's face. In conclusion, this research work determines how *"voice"* cannot be protected under the existing traditional Intellectual Property regime; therefore the scope of publicity law must expand.

• • •

Acknowledgements

I have so many people to thank in this part of my work. Professor Aakanksha Kumar and Ms. Bijetri Roy provided me with constant guidance and support throughout my journey from my initial proposal to the final draft. It was pleasure working in such a supportive environment. Both of their insights and suggestions helped me to improve my performance, research and drafting skills. I also want to thank my friends and fellow colleagues at O.P. Jindal Global University. I was a student there pursuing my Master's Degree in the subjects Intellectual Property Rights and Technology Law, year 2021-2022. I want to acknowledge my peers to provide the intellectually stimulating environment. I would like to thank Professor Aakanksha Kumar to spark my interest in the subject of Celebrity Law which further boosted my book research work. By sharing the vast knowledge Professor Kumar has amassed while working closely with various IP, Tort and Right of Publicity regulations in India and other jurisdictions, she has expanded my knowledge beyond research literature by leaps and bounds. Her valuable feedback and suggestions have been helpful and encouraging.

Last but not the least my family deserves the entire acknowledgement. My mother, Mrs. Madhuchhanda Mukherjee, my father Mr. Soumitra Mukherjee and my brother Mr. Supriyo Mukherjee are one of the most compassionate, fun and supportive family one could ever ask for. My friends Sukanya, Christy, Muskan, Samriddhi and Gauri are my forever cheerleaders and the best of friends one can surround them with. My family and friends has been a near-constant company during the writing process.

• • •

Introduction

The problem that is dealt with and discussed in this research work; the scope of Personality Rights traditionally is limited to one's *"name and likeliness"*[1] and therefore it is very narrow. It must be expanded to anything that even slightly identifies as the plaintiff. Voice is as distinctive as a person's face. The scope of personality rights must expand.

The following work is an amalgamation of various traditional Intellectual Property rights such as Copyright and Trademark. I have also discussed Tort actions such as Privacy Tort, Breach of Confidence and Defamation Tort. By the way of elimination it is determined that; *"voice is often distinctive of celebrities in the entertainment industry and other public figures like politicians, and now, social media content creators, therefore, the personality rights bundle must recognise legal protection for distinctive voice as a facet of protectable indicia."*[2] *"The deceptive aspect of this conduct has spurred plaintiffs to rely upon unfair competition and trademark law'*[3] *for relief, but without success."*[4] This study confirms that the scope of Personality Rights traditionally is limited to one's *"name and likeliness"* and therefore it is very narrow. It must be expanded to anything that even slightly identifies as the plaintiff. The scope of personality rights must expand.

The cases *"Midler*[5]*, Motschenbacher*[6]*, Carson*[7] *and Hirsch*[8]*"* are some of the landmark cases that emphasize on the expansion of the publicity rights to the entire persona of the celebrity and not just their *"name and likeliness"*[9]. These traits are the ones that the advertisers have exploited and extracted their endorsement values. Sounds and voices in the radio and television lay out a new way to the impression of celebrity endorsements. By merely using a celebrity's voice or even a song, an advertiser can create an impression of association between the celebrity and the product without even using the celebrity's face. But there is a long way to go as there are some traditionalists questioning this new idea in the name of *"name and likeliness precedent"*. Clever advertisers have been stealing away rights from celebrities who are vocally recognizable. Thus, states must open its arms to the attribute of voice within the scope of Publicity Rights and respond to the right that the law was created to prevent.

The methodology opted for this research work is *"Doctrinal"*; the analysis has been drawn out on the basis of both the *"Primary"* and the *"Secondary"* sources. The primary sources include national laws, statutes, their respective interpretations and different cases where they have been used and interpreted. The secondary sources consist of books, research papers, journals and commentaries published. All the sources have been referred based on recent legal evolution.

• • •

[1] Leonard A. Wohl, 'The Right of Publicity and Vocal Larceny: Sounding Off on SoundAlikes' [1988] 57.

[2] 'Celebrity Rights: Protection under IP Laws' (2022) <https://docs.manupatra.in/newsline/articles/Upload/78DD5FE8-5C07-4075-934D-6917CD6BE868.pdf> accessed: 24 January 2022.

[3]*SK&F, Co. v. Premo Pharmaceutical Labs. Inc.*, 625 F.2d 1055, 1065 (3d Cir. 1980).

[4]*Sinatra v. Goodyear Tire & Rubber Co.*, 435 F.2d 711 (9th Cir. 1970).

[5]*Midler v. Ford Motor Co.* 849 F.2d 460 (9th Cir. 1988).

[6]*Motschenbacher v. R.J. Reynolds Tobacco Co.* 498 F.2d 821 (9th Cir. 1974).

[7]*Carson v. Here's Johnny Portable Toilets, Inc.*, 698 F.2d 831 (6th Cir. 1983).

[8]*Hirsch v. S.C. Johnson & Son, Inc.* 90 Wis. 2d 379 (1979).

[9] Wohl (n 1).

Chapter Overview

This book has been divided into ***four different segments***;

Chapter I:"Can "voice" be a subject matter of Trademark?"

This chapter discusses various factors to determine whether "voice" can be a subject matter of Trade Mark. It discusses what exactly a Trademark is and what subject matter are covered under the Trademark law in different jurisdictions. Later on, I have discussed how does sound mark falls within the ambit of Trademark and what its essentials are. At last I conclude with explaining why "voice" cannot be registered as a "Trademark" and what problems would occur if it happens to be so.

Chapter II:"Can "voice" be a subject matter of Copyright?"

This chapter discusses various factors to determine whether "voice" can be a subject matter of Copyright. Just like the first chapter I have discussed the definition and nature of Copyright and what subject matter does the Copyright Law cover. Further with the help of a few judgements from two different jurisdictions which are not copyright voice cases per se but would help us understand the dictum behind how the subject matters like "musical works", "sound recording" and "artistic works" protects the musical elements and lyrical part of a work, but neither of them protects the voice that is heard in its entirety.

Chapter III: "Can "voice" be protected against Tort Actions?"

This chapter discusses if voice can be protected against tortious actions. I have discussed if voice rights of a celebrity can be protected under the umbrella of *Privacy*

Tort, Breach of Confidence and Defamation Tort. I have brought case studies as to how even under Tort Law it is a *"piece"* of the work that is protected and not the baritone itself. Further I have how when subjected to a quasi-contract it is only the specific *"agreen content"* that is protected and not the *"voice"*. It explains the subject matter of the right of Defamation Tort and how a likeness of the baritone is not protected. It cancels out the last option of the celebrities under which they could assert rights over their voice.

Chapter IV: "Why Right of Publicity must encompass "voice"?"

This part advocates that appropriation voice must be under the Right of Publicity in order to preserve the right of the celebrity to control the use of his/her personality. This is the concluding and the most crucial chapter of this book in this I have mentioned Publicity Rights Law in different jurisdictions and why is it necessary to expand the scope of it from mere *"name and likeliness"*[1] and include *"voice"* too. I have also discussed how various states in the United States have already recognised voice rights. In the concluding note it's been discussed how "voice" cannot be protected by the traditional Intellectual Property Rights. Thus the expansion in the scope of Right of Publicity is significant and essential.

• • •

[1] Ibid.

CHAPTER I

CAN "VOICE" BE A SUBJECT MATTER OF TRADEMARK?

1. WHAT IS A TRADEMARK?

Intellectual property is an intangible property from the human conscience and provides grounds for being awarded with legal rights. This is the case with trademarks. A trademark helps your consumers to identify you product or a service. It helps your product to stand out. A trademark can be termed as a *"valuable marketing tool"*[1] and works to *"establish brand recognition"*[2]. It differentiates your business from all other similar businesses in the industry. The recognition helps a business to grow and expand.

The United States was the first country that recognised that trademark provides us with a certain level of protections when we use it during the course of our trade in the marketplace.[3] Unfortunately, these rights and the protections are limited. An unprotected trademark can be protected in a small geographical area but when you look to expand your business in other areas, you might face difficulties if a similar trademark is already in use.[4] In order to get full protection and autonomy over a trademark it is necessary to get it registered under a concerned Trademark mechanism.

Trademark can be defined *as "a sign that is capable of being represented graphically which is capable of distinguishing goods and services of one undertaking from those of other undertakings"*[5]. But the scope of trademarks are not limited to just symbols that can be *"represented graphically"*[6], it can also be unconventional marks. Trademark owners have attained protection under various unconventional protectable subject matters like *colour* and *smell marks* subject to certain limitations.

"Trade mark" under various legislations has been defined as;

- **India: The Trade Marks Act, 1999[7];**

*"**2.(zb)** "trade mark" means a mark capable of being represented graphically and which is capable of distinguishing the goods or services of one person from those of others and may include shape of goods, their packaging and combination of colours..."*

In India, a trade mark is supposed to be *"graphically"* represented. It must distinguish the goods and services of one person from another.

- **The United States: Trademark Act of 1946[8];**

"§ 2 (15 U.S.C. § 1052)...

No trademark by which the goods of the applicant may be distinguished from the goods of others shall be refused registration on the principal register on account of its nature....."

In the United States, any mark that distinguishes one's goods and services from another can be considered to be a trademark.

- **The United Kingdom: Trade Marks Act 1994[9];**

*"**1.1)** In this Act "trade mark" means any sign which is capable—*

***(a)** of being represented in the register in a manner which enables the registrar and other competent authorities and the public to determine the clear and precise subject matter of the protection afforded to the proprietor, and*

***(b)** of distinguishing goods or services of one undertaking from those of other undertakings.*

A trade mark may, in particular, consist of words (including personal names), designs, letters, numerals, colours, sounds or the shape of goods or their packaging....."

In the United Kingdom, the purpose of a trademark remains the same, i.e. to distinguish one person's trade from another. Certain unconventional trademarks are also recognised here in the U.K. for instance, colour and smell.

- **Australia: Trade Marks Act 1995[10];**

"17.What is a trade mark?

A trade mark is a sign used, or intended to be used, to distinguish goods or services dealt with or provided in the course of trade by a person from goods or services so dealt with or provided by any other person."

Similarly, in Australia the aim and major objective of a trade mark remains constant. Trademark in the Australian legislation has been defined as any *"sign"* that is used by someone in the *"course of trade"* which distinguishes his trade from that of the other.

2. WHAT SUBJECT MATTER DOES TRADEMARK COVER?

For every Intellectual Property Right, the first question that we look into is: what subject matter does the right cover? Trademark subject matter from what we have discussed till now is the way the producer uses it and how consumers become conscious of the mark. A good trademark is a graphical and distinctive symbol of goodwill and a stamp of quality. One of the most crucial requirements for registered and unregistered trademarks is that it has to be used *"as a mark in commerce". "Distinctiveness"* is the other crucial requirement.

There are four types of Trademark namely;

i. Trademarks and Service Marks: phrases, words or symbols that defines a business's goods and services. A trademark indicates a good whereas a service mark indicates a service.
ii. Collective Mark: members of a group may benefit from a single trademark.
iii. Certificate Mark: these cover the distinctive character or a description of a product.

A phrase, word, symbol, device, scent or even a colour can be trademarked. However, the mark must be used during the course commerce. Marketing of the goods and services becomes much easier with a trademark because it assures recognition and protection of the product.

3. *WHAT ARE "SOUND MARKS" UNDER TRADEMARK?*

The Lanham Act[11] does not prohibit a sound from obtaining trademark; rather it falls under the ambit of "device". There are not many sound mark registered under the United States Patent and Trademark Office, nor cases of infringement of the same. There was one ruling which stated that a sound must be so distinctive that it gets stuck in the mind of the public, so whenever heard it must immediately associate with the source or the business. The Trademark Trial and Appeal Board has stated that in case of a sound mark the *"spectrum of distinctiveness"* must be alternative than other traditional marks. The sound must be so unique and distinctive that whenever a person listens to the sound he/she immediately associates the sound to the goods and services offered in connection to that particular sound.

Some of the sound marks registered under the United States of Patent and Trademark Office are; Pillsbury "giggle", Opening sound of the show "Law & Order", the breathing sound of Darth Vader, ESPN's "Da-da-da, da-da-da" and the whistle from the Hunger Games series. In India the first sound mark to be registered was Yahoo!'s yodel then came the Nokia tune and Britannia's 4-bell sound.

4. CAN YOU TRADEMARK A "VOICE"?

When we look at the criteria that is to be followed in order to register a trademark as discussed above, "voice" is does not fall under any of the category. Trademarks specifically covers names, logos, sounds, slogans and colours that you use during the course of trade to identify their goods and services to the public at large. A voice is a distinct personality trait of an individual which cannot be controlled by them. Thus, it would be impossible to put restrictions on the voices of the competitors.

If someone wishes to trademark a specific voice in an advertising campaign it would come under the ambit of a 'slogan' or a 'jingle'.[12] The Trademark Law will protect the said slogan or jingle but not the slogan's implementation which would include the "voice" that speaks the jingle. The baritone or the singing itself cannot be trademarked. It would not confer rights to a voice in general but will protect a few aspects like catchphrases. Amazon has recently announced the availability of Amitabh Bachchan's voice on Alexa.[13] The feature is available on all Amazon Echo devices. A mark is associated with a good or a service; in this case Amitabh Bachchan is not a good or a service. He is just selling the product or the using his voice .It is the *device* that is trademarked and not his "*voice*" per se in its entirety.

Let's assume that a celebrity is allowed to trademark their voice, this would result in legal question. For example if a singer trademarks his voice. The banner with which the artist signs a contract asks him waive his rights in return of a certain incentive. Now the company can deal with the song sung by the singer in any manner they wish without any intervention of the singer. In such a case, under what law will the song fall under? Will it be the Copyright Law or the Trademark Law? And with whom does the right lie with? Whom does it actually belong to? In the on-going Celebrity Trademark generation these questions need to be determined.

Let's assume another scenario where there is a business in India that provides some particular service. On hearing their advertisement it is very evident that the voices that are in the advertisements is of famous celebrities like Arnab Goswami, Arvind Kejriwal and Amitabh Bachchan. These celebrities are well known personalities in India and no doubt the association of these personalities with the services of the business would result in their monetary benefit. The business is surely using the likeliness of their voices. The question here is that; whether this action amount to any violation? If not trademark then under what provision can they claim relief?

5. PASSING-OFF ACTION OF TORT AND UNREGISTERED TRADEMARKS

Although there are relief designated for infringement of registered trademarks under the Trademark statutes in different jurisdictions, unregistered trademarks are also provided protection under the passing-off action claims that has been codified in various Trademark statutes. In India, "passing-off action" is not defined in The Trade Marks Act, 1999, but is referred to in Section 27(2), 134(1) and 135. The requirements to claim passing-off action has been laid down in a case *Reckitt & Colman v. Borden*[14], which are;

i. Goodwill or Reputation,
ii. Misrepresentation, and
iii. Damage.

These three requirements are together called the *"Classic Trinity"*[15]In India; *"Priority in adoption"* is given more importance than *"priority in registration"*.[16] Giving protection to unregistered trademark is a relief who wouldn't have been able to get any sort of legal remedy for the infringement of their marks.

In the United States, Section 43(A) of the Lanham Act is similar to the non-statutory common law passing-off action in the United Kingdom. In the U.S. we have a common law passing-off action because the Lanham Act got amended for which they inserted it into the statute. Section 43(A) of the Lanham Act is based in Article 10bis of the Paris Convention[17]. The Paris Convention got amended consequently the U.S. law got amended. This provides protection against "unfair competition". So, the whole idea that there can be unfair competition in the course of trade and to allow proprietors and owners of services and goods in the market an action against unfair competition practices, the Paris Convention was amended to allow for a right against unfair competition on your trade name itself.

So, the idea of "unfair competition" has been understood in several jurisdictions in many different ways in its broadest sense. The idea of "unfair competition" is a very large umbrella concept. However, passing-off claim is a "misrepresentation" style "unfair competition" claim. This "misrepresentation style of unfair competition" is codified in Section 43(A) of the Lanham Act. The 9th Circuit court in the U.S. laid down the "Sleekcraft"[18] factors to determine Passing-off claims. However, with time celebrities started to claim image rights on the grounds of "appropriation" without their authorization leading to "misrepresentation". These actions were being brought during the evolution of the "Right of Publicity" in the United States. This was before California allowed celebrities to claim "Right of Publicity" as a whole. Thus, prior to this celebrities claimed Section 43(A) in their *"name and image"*. However, "voice" was still not an option.

In the United Kingdom and Australia, passing-off is not codified. However, the term "passing off" was originally used in the U.K. In order to determine "likelihood of confusion" or whether there was "deceptive conduct" from the defendant's side, the courts examine all circumstances or impression on the consumers or their potential consumers, visual impression and judicial estimation. The test is whether the conduct of the defendant creates "confusion" to a prudent and a reasonable consumer. The Plaintiff needs to prove three elements in passing-off claim: Goodwill, misrepresentation and damage. In the *Rihanna case*[19], the U.K. court also held that the defendant and the plaintiff need not be from a common field of activity.

Passing-off action is a common law principle. The damages that are claimed under passing-off are "un-liquidated damages". The principle that it is based on is that *"a man may not sell his own goods under the pretence that they are the goods of another man."*[20] *"The passing off action depends upon the simple principle that nobody has any right to represent his goods as the goods of somebody else."*[21] Fraud must not be a necessary element of the right of action. This action applies when there is confusion between two marks and identity because of the unauthorised use of marks. It is because the main objective of the passing-off action is whether deception is likely to arise, this action can be used to protect any kind of distinctive name, mark, or logo. Voice per se is not protectable under the Trademark Law. And as a person's voice is not covered within the scope of the subject matter of trademark, the passing off action would fail to provide relief to these celebrities.

• • •

[1] 'Trademark' (2022) <https://www.law.cornell.edu/wex/trademark> accessed: 8 May 2022.

[2] Ibid.

[3] 'Trademarks in United States of America (USA) - S.S Rana & Co' (2022) <https://ssrana.in/global-ip/international-trademark-filing-registration/trademarks-in-united-states/> accessed: 8 May 2022.

[4] Ibid.

[5]*Qualitex v. Jacobsen Products Co.* [1995] 514 U.S. 159.

[6] Ibid.

[7] The Trade Marks Act, 1999.

[8] Trademark Act of 1946.

[9] Trade Marks Act 1994.

[10] Trade Marks Act 1995.

[11] Lanham (Trademark) Act.

[12] 'Can You Trademark a Voice?' (2022) <https://secureyourtrademark.com/can-you-trademark/trademark-a-voice/> accessed: 7 June 2022.

[13] 'Amazon.in: Amitabh Bachchan – celebrity voice on Alexa: Alexa Skills' (2022) <https://www.amazon.in/Amitabh-Bachchan-celebrity-voice-Alexa/dp/B092L9LQ38> accessed: 7 June 2022.

[14]*Reckitt & Colman v. Borden Inc. [1990] All E.R. 873.*

[15] Ibid.

[16]*N.R. Dongre and Ors. v Whirlpool Corporation And Anr* [1995] AIR Del 300.

[17] Paris Convention.

[18]*AMF Inc. v. Sleekcraft Boats*, 599 F.2d 341 (9th Cir. 1979).

[19]*Fenty & Ors v Arcadia Group Brands Ltd. & Anor* [2015] EWCA CIV 3.

[20] See (n 26).

[21]*ICC Development (International) Ltd. v. Arvee Enterprises* 2003 (26) PTC 245 (Del.).

CHAPTER II

CAN "VOICE" BE A SUBJECT MATTER OF COPYRIGHT?

1. WHAT IS PROTECTABLE SUBJECT MATTER UNDER COPYRIGHT?

Copyright is an Intellectual property right which protects one's literary and artistic works such as films, music, books, paintings, etc. It can be termed as the "author's right". It is the right to copy any work by the author himself or by the author's permission. The term author is used for the creator of the artistic work. In order to acquire this protection it is vital that the work should be;

i. Original work that has not been published before, and
ii. Fixated in any tangible form.

The work must be expressed in any tangible form like paper, a recording, painting, web servers, etc. in order to be copyrighted.

Copyright Law in India is governed by the *"Copyright Act, 1957"*. Under the Indian Copyright Law literary works, dramatic works, musical works, artistic works, cinematographic films and sound recordings are protected. In the United States, the Copyright Law of the States gives *"monopoly protection"* for *"original works of authorship"*[1]. In the United States, authors are given exclusive rights. These rights last for 70 years after author's death ad 95 years after the work is published. Here, the types of works protected include literary, musical, dramatic, pantomimes, graphic, sculptural, sound recording, derivative works, compilations and architectural works. In the United Kingdom, copyright is considered to be an intangible property right. It is governed by the *"Copyright, Designs and Patents Act 1988"*. Similarly, in Australia copyright is governed under the *"Copyright Act, 1968"*. These are legally enforceable rights of creators of artistic works in Australian law. Prior to year 2004, in Australia a work was said to be in public domain after fifty years of the creator's death. However, after 2004 Australia adopted the United States policy of "Plus 70" which means that the work entered the public domain after seventy years of the creator's death.

Below is the list of legislations stating the protectable subject matters in various different jurisdictions:

- **India: The Copyright Act, 1957[2];**

*"**13.** Works in which copyright subsists.— **(1)** Subject to the provisions of this section and the other provisions of this Act, copyright shall subsist throughout India in the following classes of works, that is to say,—*

*(**a**) original literary, dramatic, musical and artistic works;*

*(**b**) cinematograph films; and*

*(**c**) 1[sound recording]....."*

In Indian copyright legislation, protection has been provided to the list of subject matters mentioned above. However, it does not involve *"pantomimes or choreographic works"* separately, it is so because these works are protected within the ambit of *"cinematographic works"* itself.

- **The United States: The Copyright Act of 1976[3];**

*"**§102** · Subject matter of copyright: In general28*

***(a)**.....*

***(1)** literary works;*

***(2)** musical works, including any accompanying words;*

***(3)** dramatic works, including any accompanying music;*

***(4)** pantomimes and choreographic works;*

***(5)** pictorial, graphic, and sculptural works;*

***(6)** motion pictures and other audiovisual works;*

***(7)** sound recordings; and*

***(8)** architectural works......"*

However, unlike India, the United States have a more detailed list of subject matters that are protected under its copyright regime. It includes every work under a separate heading.

- **The United Kingdom: Copyright, Designs and Patents Act 1988[4];**

*"**1** Copyright and copyright works*

***(1)** Copyright is a property right which subsists in accordance with this Part in the following descriptions of work--*

***(a)** original literary, dramatic, musical or artistic works,*

***(b)** sound recordings, films or broadcasts, and*

***(c)** the typographical arrangement of published editions...."*

Interestingly, United Kingdom Copyright regime includes "typographical arrangement of published editions as well, which no other jurisdiction provides.

- **Australia: Copyright Act, 1968[5];**

*"**92.-(1.)** Subject to this Act, copyright subsists in a published edition of a literary, dramatic, musical or artistic*

work, or of two or more literary, dramatic, musical or artistic works...."

In Australia, the moment any idea is fixated in a tangible medium "on a paper or electronically" it is protected by copyright. Widely, the subject matter in Australia includes *"original literary, dramatic, musical and artistic works".*

To sum it up based on different jurisdictions as mentioned above, Copyright provides protection to the following works;

i. Literary works,
ii. Dramatic works,
iii. Artist works,
iv. Cinematograph films,
v. Musical works,
vi. Sound recordings,
vii. Computer software/ programs, and
viii. Architectural works.

2. CAN "VOICE" BE A SUBJECT MATTER OF COPYRIGHT?

Voice, per se cannot be copyrighted. As mentioned above, copyright provides protection only for literary, artistic, dramatic, cinematographic, musical works and records. By no means does *"voice"* fall within the ambit of all the mentioned categories. A voice can be protected only to the extent it is a part of a tangible medium such in a song, an advertisement or a movie may be copyrighted. However, copyright does not give protection specifically to voice. Although voice itself cannot be copyrighted, recordings of the voice can be copyrighted. Any oral forms of expressions are protected under the Copyright Law.[6]

There is no doubt that a few "voices" are very distinctive in nature and we tend to recognise the faces behind those voices immediately. Two very well-known actors of Bollywood; Amitabh Bachchan and Sunny Deol are one of the few people who expressed their wish to seek copyright protection for their voice. Mr. Amitabh Bachchan was vey annoyed when a Gutka company used his voice in their advertisements. He claimed that using his voice with his consent for monetary benefit and especially for a "Gutka" advertisement was illegal and unjust.[7][8] Sunny Deol in the year 2009 sent a legal notice to Big 92.7 FM's office because they used a mimic artist to mimic his and his family's voice. He also claimed that the act of airing such show with his voice was illegal.[9] But unfortunately copyright does not protect people's voices. Copyright only provides protection for literary, artistic, dramatic and musical works as per Section 13 of the Copyright Act[10].

In the United Kingdom, the Copyright, Designs and Patents Act 1988 confers rights under Section 182 to Section 184 which prohibits to record a live performance and to make copies of that recording without consent. This was held in the case *Experience Hendrix LLC v. Purple Haze Records Ltd.*[11]Thus, one could protect their voice that is fixated in any tangible medium but just their voice in isolation is not protected.

In the United States of America, actors are given various protections under the umbrella of Celebrity Rights. In the case of *Midler v. Ford Motor Co.*[12], singer Bette Midler asserted rights over her voice but the Court of Appeal held that "*.....A voice is not copyrightable. The sounds are not 'fixed'*"[13], they are granted relief under common law for "*appropriation of identity*"[14]. A person's voice in the abstract cannot be protected, but the underlying works could be. But this case is not a case of Copyright but a Publicity right case. This case did not involve copyright.

In India in the case of *"Neha Bhasin v Anand Raj Anand and Anr."*[15] "Performers rights" before the 2012 Amendment was argued. However, the Court made a very interesting point, where sound engineers were called to made distinction between two singers; Neha Bhasin and Poonam Khubani. The sound engineers were asked to submit two DCs; one without any overlaying music containing just the voice of Neha Bhasin and one with just the voice of Poonam Khubani. The Court replayed the recordings multiple times and held that it was prima facie Neha Bhasin's voice that has recorded all three versions of the song "Ek Look Ek Look" the song in question used in the movie and has credited her as a background vocalist. In this case, later on performer's rights and the interpretation of the word *"live"* were argued in the Court. In the end, Neha Bhasin's performer's rights were upheld. However, as mentioned in the judgement the Court did find the voice in the recording of the three versions of the song to be Neha Bhasin's voice. This was possible because of her *"distinctive"* voice. Neha Bhasin's performer's rights were upheld with relation to her *"voice"* in those three particular recordings. However, she cannot claim copyright over her "voice" per se. She claimed performer's right over her voice that recorded the three songs in a movie. The copyright still lies with the Producer.

Recently, a leading NFT marketplace "Diginoor" released a statement which said that it would auction a 30-minute track of the late legendary singer SP Balasubramanyam titled *"Vishwaroopa Darlsanam"*.[16] It was recorded a few weeks before the legendary singer's death due to Covid-19. 51% of the copyright will also be transferred to the NFT holder which would give them the right to reproduce the work as they wish to in the future. However, the copyright lies in "30- minute track" the "recording" and not his "voice".

Copyright provides categories that are protected such as: *"sound recording"* and *"musical works."* Both protect the musical elements and lyrical part of the work involved, but neither of them protects the voice that is heard in its entirety. It is the noise or the lyrics a voice is making that is protected, but the voice in isolation remains unprotected. There is no "idea" in a voice. In fact a voice cannot embody anything. It is the idea that is expressed in form of any noise or words or thoughts of any person that embodies an idea and hence is protectable under the Copyright Law. In the case, *Butler v. Target Corp*[17]. it was held that it is the lyrics of a song that are copyrightable and not the voice uttering them. As the *"sounds are not fixed"*[18], copyright protection is not available to the words a person may utter in their distinctive voice.

• • •

[1] (2022) <https://www.supremecourt.gov/opinions/19pdf/18-1150_7m58.pdf> accessed: 7 June 2022.

[2] The Copyright Act, 1957.

[3] The Copyright Act 1976.

[4] Copyright, Designs and Patents Act 1988.

[5] Copyright Act 1968.

[6] 'When celebrities seek copyrights' (2022) <https://www.financialexpress.com/archive/when-celebrities-seek-copyrights/729569/> accessed: 7 May 2022.

[7] 'Amitabh Bachchan sends legal notice to pan masala brand as ads continue to air despite contract termination' (2022) <https://indianexpress.com/article/entertainment/bollywood/amitabh-bachchan-sends-legal-notice-to-pan-masala-brand-as-ads-continue-to-air-despite-contract-termination-7633125/> accessed: 8 May 2022.

[8] 'Mail Today. Amitabh Bachchan to get copyright' (2022) available at: <https://www.indiatoday.in/movies/celebrities/story/amitabh-bachchan-to-get-copyright-85190-2010-11-08> accessed: 8 May 2022.

[9] 'When celebrities seek copyrights' (2022) <https://www.financialexpress.com/archive/when-celebrities-seek-copyrights/729569/> accessed: 8 May 2022.

[10] The Copyright Act, 1957.

[11]*Experience Hendrix LLC v. Purple Haze Records Ltd.* [2007] EWCA Civ 501.

[12]*Midler v. Ford Motor Co.* 849 F.2d 460 (9th Cir. 1988).

[13] Ibid.

[14] Ibid.

[15]*Neha Bhasin v Anand Raj Anand and Anr.* Delhi HC 20 April, 2006.

[16] 'Diginoor to launch NFT of SP Balasubrahmanyam's unreleased song' (2022) <https://www.thehindubusinessline.com/news/diginoor-to-launch-nfts-of-sp-balasubrahmanyams-unreleased-song/article65267411.ece> accessed: 14 June 2022.

[17]*Butler v. Target Corporation,* 323 F. Supp. 2d 1052 (C.D. Cal. 2004).

[18] Ibid.

CHAPTER III

TORT AND "VOICE INDICIA": CAN VOICE BE PROTECTED AGAINST TORT ACTIONS?

1. WHAT IS PRIVACY?

Privacy has not been defined under any legal statute, thus making it a very vague concept. "Privacy" can be termed as "exasperatingly vague and evanescent"[1]. This "Right to Privacy" in an article authored by "Louis Brandeis and Samuel D. Warren" called for the recognition of a *"right to be left alone"*[2], stating that *"privacy was part of the more general right to the immunity of the person, the right to one's personality"*[3]. "Right to Privacy" protects individuals from unwanted exposure and publicity in the press.[4] In the United States of America this is common law right. It can be easily claimed by the First Amendment, given that it has constitutional status. In the "European Convention of Human Rights"[5], Article 8 which talks about "The Right to Privacy"[6] and Article 10 "Freedom of expression"[7] has acquired equal constitutional status. Right to Privacy has been enshrined in the U.S. Constitution[8] and as well as under Article 21 of the Constitution of India[9]. However, in different jurisdictions like in the U.K. and Australia, courts are reluctant in recognising the "Privacy Tort". They rely on other mechanisms like the "passing-off tort" or "defamation tort", in countries like U.K. and E.U. "Breach of Confidence" tort is also referred to.

1.1. WHETHER "*VOICE INDICIA*" CAN BE PROTECTED UNDER AN INVASION TORT ACTION?

The Tort of invasion of privacy does not exist per se. Lord Hoffman in a case states that, "*There are a number of common law and statutory remedies of which it may be said that one at least of the underlying values they protect is a right of privacy. [...] Common law torts include trespass, nuisance, defamation and malicious falsehood; there is the equitable action for breach of confidence and statutory remedies under the Protection from Harassment Act 1997 and the Data Protection Act 1998"*[10]. There exist a number of legal mechanisms which can be argued in order to protect one's privacy. Mere absence of tort of invasion of privacy does not mean that there is no argument for such an invasion. Doctrine of breach of confidence and Defamation tort comes into play whenever such cases occur.

William Lloyd Prosser in an article[11] threw some more light on the views of Brandeis and Warren[12] and lays down four categories under which invasion of Privacy can be succumbed:

"***(1)*** *Intrusion upon the plaintiff's seclusion or solitude or into private affairs*

(2) *Public disclosure of embarrassing private facts about the plaintiff;*

(3)*Publicity which places the plaintiff in a false light in the public eye; and*

(4) *Appropriations for the defendant's advantage of the plaintiff's name or likeness."*[13]

1.2. PRIVACY TORT AND RIGHT TO PUBLICITY

In the beginning private individuals began file appropriation cases for mental suffering due to their unauthorised use of likeness commercially. Soon public figures began to file similar cases order to seek remuneration for unauthorised use of their persona, rather than damages for mental agony and suffering from the unwanted exposure or publicity. The Courts began to distinguish Privacy rights from the Publicity rights soon after this.

1.3. PRIVACY TORT AND "*VOICE INDICIA*"

From the above analysis we can conclude that "Privacy" is argued when there is a question of one's dignity, Kantian autonomy and inviolate personality.[14] And a person's "*voice*" does not come under the ambit of any of the above interests. Privacy cases involves disclosure of information that are highly offensive causing mental agony and suffering which does not concern the public or cases where an individual is portrayed in a bad light in the eye of public. Moreover, these offences are covered under different other legal mechanisms like Disclosure, breach of contract and the defamation tort.

However, if a public person claims remuneration for mental agony due to release of some private information, for example a sound recording, it will the recording which would be in question. The individual cannot claim the right of invasion of privacy for the usage of his voice in the sound recording in question. The baritone of his voice is not protectable.

In the case *Michaels v Internet Entertainment Group Inc.[15]*, a video was in question which depicted Bret Michaels and Pamela Anderson Lee having sexual intercourse. The Court in this case held in favour of the plaintiff saying that "*Sexual relations are among the most personal and intimate of acts. The Court is not prepared to conclude that public exposure of one sexual encounter forever removes a person's privacy interest in all subsequent and previous sexual encounters".[16]* "*The fact that she has performed a role involving sex does not, however, make her real sex life open to the public."*[17] *"Where the publicity is so offensive as to constitute a morbid and sensational prying into private lives for its own sake, it serves no legitimate public interest and is not deserving of protection."*[18]

Similarly, now let's suppose instead of a video it was an audio sex tape, the Court would still have held the same because it would have been a female's voice in that recording exposing one's sexual encounter which is highly offensive. However, the injunction and protection would have been granted for the *"audio tape"* or the *"sound recording"* as a whole. *"Voice"* in its entirety would still not hold any prerogative.

2. BREACH OF CONFIDENCE TORT

The doctrine or the tort of Breach of Confidence can be defined as a category under which protection of one's privacy is guaranteed which offers damages if there is a violation of privacy. *"The action for breach of confidence is now being used as the basis for regular orders by the courts with the clear aim and effect of affording a remedy against unauthorised publication of personal information by the media."*[19] The Courts have determined that there must be a balance between Article 8 and Article 10 of the European Convention on Human Rights[20]. The four major subject matters that the Breach of Confidence Tort protects are; trade secrets, personal confidences, artistic and literary confidences and government information. In order to build a case of Breach of Confidence it is important to fulfil four elements: firstly, there must be some confidential information; secondly, the defendant should be under an obligation to not to disclose the confidential information;

thirdly, the act of use or disclosure of the information is in breach of the obligation of confidentiality; lastly, the defendant may take up the "public interest defence" which states that the disclosed information was in public interest.

In the case *Campbell v Mirror*[21], the court laid down two-part test to determine Breach of Confidence:

(1) Whether the information is private to the plaintiff?

"If the information is obviously private, the situation will be one where the person to whom it relates can reasonably expect his privacy to be respected. So there is normally no need to go on and ask whether it would be highly offensive for it to be published."[22]

(2) Whether the benefits of the disclosure of the information proportionate to the harm that is caused to the plaintiff due to the invasion of privacy?

"They are whether publication of the material pursues a legitimate aim and whether the benefits that will be achieved by its publication are proportionate to the harm that may be done by the interference with the right to privacy."[23]

In another case *Von Hannover v Germany*[24], the Court held that the scope of private life extends to one's identity like their name, photo and physical or moral integrity. The Court in order to attain balance between *"right to privacy"* and *"freedom of speech and expression"* by following relevant criteria;

*"**(1)** Contribution to a debate of general interest.*

***(2)** How well known is the person concerned and what is the subject of the report.*

***(3)** Prior conduct of the person concerned.*

***(4)** Content, form and consequence of the publication.*

***(5)** Circumstance in which the photo was taken."*[25]

To understand our above discussion better let's take an example; let's suppose a media house publishes a series of voice recordings of a famous public figure talking about their private affairs which has nothing to do with public interest. If the Court finds that the "sound recording" that is published results in the invasion of privacy of the public figure or the celebrity, then the defendants will be held liable of invading their privacy with respect to the "sound recording" and not the baritone of the voice in the recording no matter how distinctive the voice is. The right of the public figure lies in their "privacy" that has been breached. In no way their "voice" prima facie can be protected under this tort.

2.1. BREACH OF CONFIDENCE AND *"VOICE"* INDICIA

As per our discussion now we know what is a *"Breach of Confidence"* Tort, what all the subject matters are protected under this tort and elements to establish this breach. Breach of Confidence Tort protects an individual from invasion of their privacy. Article 8 of the European Convention on Human Rights bestows us with the *"Right to Respect for private and family life"* which protect an individual's life and family from any sort of interference in order to protect their privacy.

This refers to any kind of information which is actually used or is disclosed. This information in question can be a picture or multiple pictures, a written article, a video or even a sound recording. But again it is the *"particular content"* that is in question and not the tone of the voice. Mere the presence of an individual's *"voice"* cannot be a ground of the claim of "Breach of Confidence" Tort.

3. DEFAMATION TORT

The term *"Defamation"* can be defined as *"communication that tends to harm the reputation of another to lower his estimation in the community or deter third parties from associating with him"*[26]. Law protects people from different kinds of harm which also includes their name and character. A statement that is made orally or in a written format which tends to have a negative impact on a person's reputation in the community, then that statement is deemed to be defamatory. *"Defamation means the act of communicating false statements about a person that injure the reputation of that person."*[27]It thus injures the person's character and fame. Everyone has the right against invasion of his reputation. Defamation is divided into categories one is *"Libel"* and the other is *"Slander"*. "Libel" is when the statement is made in a fixed medium which means it is either written or printed. Whereas, *"slander"* is when the defamatory statement is made in a non-fixed medium or orally.[28]

3.1. DEFAMATION IN DIFFERENT JURISDICTIONS

In India under Section 499 of the Indian Penal Code[29] is defined "Defamation". It states that "by words either spoken or intended to be read, or by signs or by visible representations, to make or publish any imputation concerning any person intending to harm, or knowing or having reason to believe that such imputation will harm, the reputation, of such person"[30]. In India, cases of defamation can be filed under the criminal as well as civil law.[31] Defamation Law in India is very similar to that of the U.K. Tort Law. Indian courts in terms to defences against a Defamation suit have recognised the defence of *"absolute"*[32] and *"qualified privilege"*[33], *"fair comment"*[34] and *"justification"*[35]. The punishment for such offence is imprisonment for upto two years or fine or both. In the recent times a lot of cases have been in light with relation to defamation cases where the reputation of a public figure has been tarnished.

The history of Defamation in England is very vague. It goes back to the times of Edward I (1272-1307). The modern Tort law in the U.K. and Ireland has descended from the traditional English defamation law. Defamation Tort is a civil wrong in these Jurisdictions. Defamation cases in England are heard in the High Court.[36] The defences available are *"absolute and qualified privilege, fair comment and justification"[37]*. The burden of proof lies with the Defendant. However, in order to collect damages it is the public figure must prove that the act of disclosure of the information was malicious. Defamation under Criminal Law in the U.K. was abolished by Section 73 of the Coroners and Justice Act, 2009[38]. It was reformed by the enactment of the Defamation Act, 2013[39].

Defamation in the United States can be defined as a *"communication that tends to harm the reputation of another to lower his estimation in the community or deter third parties from associating with him"*[40]. A statement is deemed as defamatory if there is a negative impact on a person's reputation in a community even if the number of the persons impacted does not form a majority in that community.[41] The level of defamation differs from case to case. In order to file a Defamation suit in the U.S. it is necessary to fulfil the following four criterias; firstly, the statement published must be a false one; secondly, it must be defamatory; thirdly, the statement must be published to a third party; lastly, there must be harm to the claimant's reputation.[42] In order to prove Defamation, it is important to prove that the statement made must be a false one and not in public interest. If the Defendant succeeds in proving that the publication was an innocent one where they has reasonable grounds to believe that the statement is true then it is not considered to be defamatory.[43]

The Australian Defamation Law is based on and similar to the English Tort Law. In the case *Duffy v. Google*[44], Justice Blue summarized the new Australian Defamation Law. He said that the Defamation tort can be divided into five parts; firstly; the defendants must publish the statement to a third party; secondly; the defamatory work must be defamatory in nature; thirdly, the passage must be an information; fourth, the information must be about the plaintiff; lastly, there must be a damage to the plaintiff's reputation.[45]

In India, there is also a provision under which a defamation suit can be brought by a deceased person's relative for a defamatory imputation against the deceased person which damaged or harmed his name and reputation.[46] However, under the U.S. common law it is stated that a deceased person cannot be defamed therefore, no protection is granted for the same as "the dead does not have reputations to damage"[47] . Similarly, in the United Kingdom the dead cannot be defamed because defamation there is considered to be a personal action which cannot be brought up by someone else. A libel action by the relatives of the deceased person was attempted in the "Defamation Act 2013"[48] but it was defeated.[49] Although there is no common law right against "Defamation" in Australia, the six different states have their own laws for defamation. However, there is no provision of a suit against defamation of a deceased person in any of the states in Australia because of the same reason that it is a personal action which cannot be brought up any anybody else.[50]

3.2. SUBJECT MATTER OF DEFAMATION

From the multiple definitions of the "Defamation Tort" it can be derived that, it is an oral or a written statement that is published in the community which causes harm to the reputation of the person the statement is made about. In multiple jurisdictions, multiple criterias are laid down by the statutes and the Court judgements explaining what constitutes a Defamation Tort Law suit. The same can be summarised in the following elements:

i. The statement publishes should be a false statement;
ii. It must be defamatory to the plaintiff;
iii. The statement must be published in a community; and
iv. There must be damage to the reputation of the plaintiff.

Everybody has the right to protect their name and reputation. And Defamation Tort is the mechanism that helps people to protect the same. Public figures are more prone to defamatory statements as they are constantly in the public spotlight. Indeed it is important for the media to bring into light the matters concerning to public interest in light, but there must be a balance.[51] Defamation Tort provides the balance. This legal mechanism has become the spine of the right to protection of one's good name and reputation.

3.3. CAN *"VOICE"* BE PROTECTED UNDER THE DEFAMATION TORT?

The world famous Bollywood Actor with the most distinctive voice recently in the year 2010 tried to claim copyright over the baritone of his unbeatable voice.[52] Mr. Bachchan was very annoyed with a Gutka brand who used a voice over which sounded like him with his authorization. He claimed it to be *"disgusting, unethical and wrong"*[53]. But after our discussion in Chapter 2 of this research work book, we know that copyright cannot be claimed for anyone's "voice". But in the light of this matter Mr. Amitabh Bachchan can claim damages under the Defamation law enumerated under *"Section 499 of the Indian Penal Code, 1860"***[54]**. This claim would satisfy all the four elements necessary for a defamation suit. Firstly, the advertisement was made in such a way that made people to believe Mr. Bachchan's association with the brand. Secondly, the fact that Amitabh Bachchan is a big name in our country who does not consume tobacco in any form neither does he promote smoking, makes the advertisement defamatory. Thirdly, the advertisement was released for the public to see. And lastly, it did harm Mr. Bachchan's reputation.[55]

Defamation suit can also be filed in case of a deceased person on the ground that the imputation harmed the deceased person's name, fame and honour.[56] The next of kin or the person's partner could claim defamation and bring suit against it.[57] But if the above explained scenario occurs where the imputation in question is the person's "voice", then such a claim cannot be entertained under the Defamation Tort. For instance, if some brand uses the voice of Late legendary actor Dilip Kumar which his wife Saira Bano finds to be Defamatory to his name or honour, she can bring a suit against it.[58] This would protect his honour but not his "voice" per se.

From the above analysis we can conclude that, Defamation Tort is a legal mechanism used to claim protection against invasion of right to good name and reputation. It helps protect people both civil and public figures from their reputation being tarnished wrongfully. However, it does not protect a likeness of the baritone of a voice. It is designed to solely protect one's name and reputation in a community.

• • •

[1] Arthur R. Miller, 'The Assault on Privacy: Computers' [1971] 4.

[2] Louis Brandeis, Samuel D. Warren, 'The Right to Privacy' [1890] 4 Harvard Law Review.

[3] Ibid.

[4] Ibid.

[5] European Convention on Human Rights, 1950.

[6] Ibid.

[7] Ibid.

[8] The Constitution of the United States of America.

[9] The Constitution of India, 1950.

[10] *Wainwright v Home Office* [2004] 2 AC 406.

[11] William L. Prosser, Privacy, 48 CAL. L. REV. 383 (1960).

[12] Brandeis (n 50).

[13] Prosser (n 59).

[14] Ibid.

[15] *Michaels v. Internet Entertainment Group, Inc.*, 5 F.Supp.2d 823 (C.D. Cal. 1998).

[16] Ibid.

[17] Ibid.

[18] Ibid.

[19] Gavin Phillipson, 'Transforming Breach of Confidence? Towards a Common Law Right of Privacy under the Human Rights Act' [2003] 5 The Modern Law Review.

[20] European Convention on Human Rights, 1950.

[21] *Campbell v Mirror Group Newspapers* [2004] UKHL 22.

[22] Ibid.

[23] Ibid.

[24]*Von Hannover v Germany* [2012] ECtHR.

[25] Ibid.

[26] The Restatement (Second) of Torts, s 509.

[27] 'Defamation' (2022) <https://www.merriam-webster.com/dictionary/defamation> accessed: 8 May 2022.

[28] 'Defamation: Libel and Slander | ExpertLaw' (2022). <https://www.expertlaw.com/library/personal_injury/defamation.html> accessed: 8 May 2022.

[29] The Indian Penal Code, 1860.

[30] Ibid.

[31] 'The Hindu: Opinion / Leader Page Articles: Defamation litigation: a survivor's kit' (2022) <https://web.archive.org/web/20130722120816/http://www.hindu.com/2004/09/21/stories/2004092103551000.htm> accessed: 8 May 2022.

[32]*Pukhraj v. State of Rajasthan* [1973] SCC (Cri) 944.

[33]*Rustom K. Karanjia and Anr v Krishnaraj M.D. Thackersey and Ors.* [1970] 72 BOMLR 94.

[34]*Ram Jethmalani v. Subramaniam Swamy* [2006] (87) DRJ 603.

[35]*Santosh Tewari and Ors v. State of U.P. and Anr* [1996] (20) ACR 808.

[36] Douglas W. Vick, Linda Macpherson, 'An Opportunity Lost: The United Kingdom's Failed Reform of Defamation Law' [1997] 49.

[37] 'Wayback Machine' (2022) <https://web.archive.org/web/20140209044821/http://a4id.org/sites/default/files/user/Legal%20Guide_defamation.pdf> accessed: 8 May 2022).

[38] Coroners and Justice Act 2009.

[39] Defamation Act 2013.

[40] The Restatement (Second) of Torts, s 509.

[41] The Restatement (Second) of Torts, s 559 comment e.

[42] The Restatement (Second) of Torts, §558.

[43]*Gertz v. Robert Welch, Inc.* [1974] 418 U.S. 323.

[44]*Duffy v. Google Inc.* [2015] SASC 170.

[45] Ibid.

[46] The Indian Penal Code, s 499.

[47] 'Can You Defame & Slander a Dead Person?' (2022) <https://www.minclaw.com/legal-resource-center/what-is-defamation/can-dead-people-defamed/?> accessed: 10 May 2022.

[48] Defamation Act 2013.

[49] 'Can you defame the dead?' (2022) <https://www.lexisnexis.co.uk/blog/wipit/can-you-defame-the-dead> accessed: 10 May 2022.

[50] Gotz Bottner, 'Protection of the Honour of Deceased Persons - A Comparison Between the German and the Australian Legal Situation' [2001] 5 Bond Law Review 109.

[51] 'Tort Law: The Rules of Defamation' (2022) available at: <https://lawshelf.com/shortvideoscontentview/tort-law-the-rules-of-defamation> accessed: 8 May 2022.

[52] 'Mail Today. Amitabh Bachchan to get copyright' (2022) available at: <https://www.indiatoday.in/movies/celebrities/story/amitabh-bachchan-to-get-copyright-85190-2010-11-08> accessed: 8 May 2022.

[53] Ibid.

[54] The Indian Penal Code, 1860.

[55] 'Bachchan: Amitabh Bachchan scraps advertisement contract with pan masala brand | Mumbai News - Times of India' (2022) available at:

<https://timesofindia.indiatimes.com/city/mumbai/mumbai-big-b-scraps-ad-contract-with-pan-masala-brand/articleshow/86949662.cms> accessed: 8 May 2022.

[56] The Indian Penal Code, s 499.

[57] Ibid.

[58] 'Dilip Kumar, Saira Banu send defamation notice to builder' (2022) <https://indianexpress.com/article/entertainment/bollywood/dilip-kumar-saira-banu-defamation-notice-5523712/> accessed: 8 June 2022.

CHAPTER IV

WHY RIGHT OF PUBLICITY MUST ENCOMPASS "VOICE"?

1. NATURE AND SCOPE OF RIGHT OF PUBLICITY IN DIFFERENT JURISDICTIONS

Right of Publicity can also be termed as Personality Rights. This right gives an individual the right to control the use of their identity commercially. This identity may include an individual's name, likeness, image or anything that identifies as him. These are the rights that give individuals right to exploit and use commercial gains from the use of their name, likeness and persona.

In Australia, right of publicity can claimed under "passing-off" tort action. In the *Henderson case*[1], the plaintiffs were ballroom dancers and they claimed rights over their image which was used without their authorization on a cover of a gramophone record. They claimed their right under passing-off tort action. United Kingdom does not recognise Right of Publicity. It does not have a legal statute that would protect a person's name, likeness or image. There is no way that one could protect their personality or identity from unauthorized commercial exploitation. However, one may claim protection in the U.K. under various intellectual property law regime and tort. It can be indirectly protected through copyright law, trademark law, and passing-off tort. One can also claim Defamation and Malicious falsehood. However, the Court in the *Elvis Presley case* fails to offer an appropriate level of protection. Similarly, in India the concept of Publicity Rights is not very clear. There is no specific legislation or statute that governs the same. However, recently the Madras High Court in the *Rajnikant case*[2] passed an injunction against a movie "Main Hoon Rajnikant". The court in this case held that using Rajnikant's name without his authorization violated is reputation and goodwill in his name. This way the Court upheld Publicity rights in India. A few High Courts have tried to recognise Publicity Rights as a standalone right. It was in another case of *ICC Development*[3], where it was held that publicity rights evolve from one's right to privacy and that it can be with respect to an individual's name, personality and signature. In India, right to privacy is enshrined under Article 21 of the Constitution of India.

However, in the United States Publicity Rights have been codified in various states. It protects commercial value of identity of an individual. It is considered to be a property right. It is recognised in Common Law and Statutes in majority of the states. The three main elements to look for in the United States while claiming Right of Publicity are; Use of identity, which means taking of name and likeness which would identify as the plaintiff; second, whether the defendant gain any commercial benefit; lastly, whether the defendant can plea the First Amendment defence which is use of the name and likeness for the purposes of news, political speech, critical commentary, etc. We will focus more on New York and California because major chunk of celebrities live there.

In New York, it has been codified as a part of "Right of Publicity" under *"Article 5 of the New York Civil Rights*

Law". New York does not have a separate common law right of publicity. Sections 50 and 51 also describe similar rights but different mechanisms. Section 50 makes it violation of misdemeanour and Section 51 provides a private cause of action. Section 51 provides protection to one's name, portrait, picture and voice. However, new legislation which entered into force on 29 May 2021 as a new Section 50(f) to the Civil Rights Law titled "Right of Publicity". In the case *"Midler v. Ford Motor Co."*[4], actress and singer Bette Midler was asked to record the song "Do You Wanna Dance" for a commercial. When she refused the defendant used a sound-alike to imitate the song and misled the listeners into believing that it was Midler's "voice". This is California 9th Circuit case, where a celebrity's distinctive and known voice was intentionally imitated in order to sell a product, the sellers appropriated her "voice" and committed a tort in California. California has a common law right of publicity that lays down the passage of the statutory right and it remains valid and additive.[5] Even California provides civil claim for unauthorised use of another's "name, voice, signature, photograph or likeness".

2. WHY RIGHT OF PUBLICITY MUST EXTEND TO "VOICE"?

From the above discussion we can conclude that unlike in the United States, Right of Publicity is still a very elusive concept in some countries and has a long way to go ahead. However, interestingly when we discussed the Right of Publicity in the United States we observed that it provides claim for protection over an individual's "voice" not only in California but also in thirteen other states. Thus, expansion of the scope of right of publicity is possible. Further, I will establish the value of an individual's voice by discussing a few instances; Why was Amitabh Bachchan's voice used in the new Alexa?; Why are there audio books recorded in various widely known individual's voice?; Why was Amitabh Bachchan's voice used in the Covid-19 caller tune?; Why do we immediately think of Pandit Jawaharlal Nehru when we listen to the "Tryst with Destiny" speech?

Answer to these questions is because "voice" plays a very distinctive factor in our lives. We associate people on the basis of their voices. Gone are the days when just videos held an advertising and commercial value. Nowadays the audio market is immensely growing. Even "voices" hold a commercial value. Therefore, now the commercial value of "voice" is divorced from just video. Celebrities have huge commercial values and so do their identifiable elements. It is not just restricted to their name and likeness it also includes their "voice". And where there is market, the potential and possibility of litigation over voice indicia is not remote. And in order to curb and manage the occurrence of such instances it is important for us to expand the limited and the traditional scope of Right of Publicity from just "name and likeness" to individual's "voices" as well because they hold the same distinguishable and commercial value.

• • •

[1]*Henderson v Radio Corp Pty Ltd*, (1960) 60 SR(NSW) 576, [1969] RPC 218.

[2]*Mr.Shivaji Rao Gaikwad v. M/S.Varsha Productions* 2015 (62) PTC 351 (Madras).

[3]*ICC Development (International) Ltd v Arvee Enterprises* 2003 (26) PTC 245.

[4] See (n 5).

[5]*Comedy III Productions, Inc. v. Gary Saderup, Inc.* (2001) 25 Cal.4th 387.

Conclusion

A celebrity, according to popular conception, is a person who has achieved widespread recognition and recognition in society, allowing him or her to be readily recognised by others. For example, in a nation like India, it might be connected with the praise and honour given to a huge number of people for some type of achievement.[1] This may also be regarded in a business context; for example, if a person's reputation is utilised to promote a product, that person will be deemed a celebrity in the sense of publicity under the "direct commercial exploitation of identity" test.[2] Celebrity rights, in conjunction with the personality they have, have the potential to have a significant impact on the general public. In such a case, it is important to recognise the efforts that have been made over many years to construct the structure, unless the situation was unexpectedly brought about by an unexpected event. In both circumstances, the commercial values connected with the individual might be quite high, and as a result, the rights under consideration can be regarded to constitute his or her Personality Rights.

Further as I have discussed multiple times earlier in my book, a person's "voice" is as distinctive as his/her face. Publicity rights provide protection to solely one's name and personality traits. Now the right has been used to *"redress the appropriation of the voice of a popular singer"*[3]. *"Voice is often distinctive of celebrities in the entertainment industry and other public figures like politicians, and now, social media content creators, therefore, the personality rights bundle must recognise legal protection for distinctive voice as a facet of protectable indicia"*[4] California is the only state that grants protection to someone's voice, but it only provides protection to the artist's voice and does not prohibit the imitation of the voice. However, because of the term *"likeliness"* that is used in the statute it can be interpreted that it includes vocal imitation too. In California, the common law has been open to one's publicity rights claims. In the case *"Midler v. Ford Motor Co."*[5], actress and singer Bette Midler was asked to record the song "Do You Wanna Dance" for a commercial. When she refused the defendant used a sound-alike to imitate the song and misled the listeners into believing that it was Midler's voice. The case of *"Motschenbacher v R.J. Reynolds Tobacco Co"* was used to explain how it was an infringement of Midler's rights by the appropriation of her identity which was her *"voice"* in this case. It was stated that in both the cases a person's attribute was stolen that could identify the plaintiffs, resulting in extraction of their endorsement value. Midler set strong case for the infringement of publicity rights by the appropriation of voice for future plaintiffs.

In this book I have discussed various instances proving that a celebrity's "voice" adds onto his/her identity. Therefore, it must be protected. In the first Chapter I discussed factors to determine whether it can be a subject matter of Trade Mark. In the second Chapter, I discussed how "voice" cannot be a part of protectable subject matter of Copyright. The third Chapter discusses if voice can be protected against tortious actions. Final Chapter advocates that "appropriation of voice" must be under the Right of Publicity to protect the rights of the celebrity to control the use of his/her personality. All of this, I have done with respect to multiple jurisdiction like the United States, United Kingdom, Australia and India. This research work/ book is a comparative study. Various States in the United

States have already recognised voice rights. In my view, the scope of Right of Publicity must expand from mere “name and likeness” to a celebrity’s “voice”. The scope must recognise anything that is slightly identical as the plaintiff. This research work proves that “voice” cannot be protected under any of the traditional Intellectual Property Rights Law regime, even under Tort Law. Thus, the expansion in the scope of Right of Publicity with respect to “voice” is essential.

• • •

[1] ‘Celebrity Rights in India’ Legal Services India <http://www.legalserviceindia.com/article/l139-Celebrity-Rights.html> accessed 16 January 2022.

[2]*Martin Luther King Jr. Centre for Social Change v American Heritage Products* 694 F2d 674.

[3] See (n 1).

[4] See (n 2).

[5] See (n 5).

References

CASES

1. AMF Inc. v. Sleekcraft Boats, 599 F.2d 341 (9th Cir. 1979)
2. Arthur R. Miller, 'The Assault on Privacy: Computers' [1971] 4
3. Butler v. Target Corporation, 323 F. Supp. 2d 1052 (C.D. Cal. 2004)
4. Campbell v Mirror Group Newspapers [2004] UKHL 22
5. Carson v. Here's Johnny Portable Toilets, Inc., 698 F.2d 831 (6th Cir. 1983)
6. Comedy III Productions, Inc. v Gary Saderup, Inc. (2001) 25 Cal.4th 387
7. Duffy v. Google Inc. [2015] SASC 170
8. Experience Hendrix LLC v. Purple Haze Records Ltd. [2007] EWCA Civ 501
9. Fenty & Ors v Arcadia Group Brands Ltd. & Anor [2015] EWCA CIV 3
10. Gertz v. Robert Welch, Inc. [1974] 418 U.S. 323
11. Henderson v Radio Corp Pty Ltd, (1960) 60 SR (NSW) 576, [1969] RPC 218
12. Hirsch v. S.C. Johnson & Son, Inc. 90 Wis. 2d 379 (1979)
13. ICC Development (International) Ltd v Arvee Enterprises 2003 (26) PTC 245
14. Martin Luther King Jr. Centre for Social Change v American Heritage Products 694 F2d 674
15. Michaels v. Internet Entertainment Group, Inc., 5 F.Supp.2d 823 (C.D. Cal. 1998)
16. Midler v. Ford Motor Co. 849 F.2d 460 (9th Cir. 1988)
17. Motschenbacher v. R.J. Reynolds Tobacco Co. 498 F.2d

821 (9th Cir. 1974)

18. Mr. Shivaji Rao Gaikwad v. M/Varsha Productions 2015 (62) PTC 351 (Madras)
19. N.R. Dongre and Ors. v Whirlpool Corporation And Anr [1995] AIR Del 300
20. Neha Bhasin v Anand Raj Anand and Anr. Delhi HC 20 April, 2006
21. Pukhraj v. State of Rajasthan [1973] SCC (Cri) 944
22. Qualitex v. Jacobsen Products Co. [1995] 514 U.S. 159
23. Ram Jethmalani v. Subramaniam Swamy [2006] (87) DRJ 603
24. Reckitt & Colman v. Borden Inc. [1990] All E.R. 873
25. Rustom K. Karanjia and Anr v Krishnaraj M.D. Thackersey and Ors. [1970] 72 BOMLR 94
26. Santosh Tewari and Ors v. State of U.P. and Anr [1996] (20) ACR 808
27. Sinatra v. Goodyear Tire & Rubber Co., 435 F.2d 711 (9th Cir. 1970)
28. SK&F, Co. v. Premo Pharmaceutical Labs. Inc., 625 F.2d 1055, 1065 (3d Cir. 1980)
29. Von Hannover v Germany [2012] ECtHR
30. Wainwright v Home Office [2004] 2 AC 406
31. William L. Prosser, Privacy, 48 CAL. L. REV. 383 (1960)

LEGISLATIONS

1. Copyright Act 1968
2. Copyright, Designs and Patents Act 1988
3. Coroners and Justice Act 2009
4. Defamation Act 2013
5. European Convention on Human Rights, 1950
6. Lanham (Trademark) Act
7. Paris Convention

8. The Constitution of India, 1950
9. The Constitution of the United States of America
10. The Copyright Act 1976
11. The Copyright Act, 1957
12. The Indian Penal Code, 1860
13. The Restatement (Second) of Torts
14. The Trade Marks Act, 1999
15. Trade Marks Act 1994
16. Trade Marks Act 1995
17. Trademark Act of 1946

RESEARCH PAPERS

1. Bottner Gotz, 'Protection of the Honour of Deceased Persons - A Comparison Between the German and the Australian Legal Situation' [2001] 5 Bond Law Review 109
2. Brandeis Louis, Samuel D. Warren, 'The Right to Privacy' [1890] 4 Harvard Law Review
3. Phillipson Gavin, 'Transforming Breach of Confidence? Towards a Common Law Right of Privacy under the Human Rights Act' [2003] 5 The Modern Law Review.
4. Vick W. Douglas W., Linda Macpherson, 'An Opportunity Lost: The United Kingdom's Failed Reform of Defamation Law' [1997] 49
5. Wohl A. Leonard, 'The Right of Publicity and Vocal Larceny: Sounding Off on SoundAlikes' [1988] 57

WEBSITES

1. (2022) <https://www.supremecourt.gov/opinions/19pdf/18-1150_7m58.pdf> accessed: 7 June 2022
2. 'Amazon.in: Amitabh Bachchan – celebrity voice on

Alexa: Alexa Skills' (2022) <https://www.amazon.in/Amitabh-Bachchan-celebrity-voice-Alexa/dp/B092L9LQ38> accessed: 7 June 2022

3. 'Amitabh Bachchan sends legal notice to pan masala brand as ads continue to air despite contract termination' (2022) <https://indianexpress.com/article/entertainment/bollywood/amitabh-bachchan-sends-legal-notice-to-pan-masala-brand-as-ads-continue-to-air-despite-contract-termination-7633125/> accessed: 8 May 2022
4. 'Bachchan: Amitabh Bachchan scraps advertisement contract with pan masala brand | Mumbai News - Times of India' (2022) available at: <https://timesofindia.indiatimes.com/city/mumbai/mumbai-big-b-scraps-ad-contract-with-pan-masala-brand/articleshow/86949662.cms> accessed: 8 May 2022
5. 'Can You Defame & Slander a Dead Person?' (2022) <https://www.minclaw.com/legal-resource-center/what-is-defamation/can-dead-people-defamed/?> accessed: 10 May 2022.
6. 'Can you defame the dead?' (2022) <https://www.lexisnexis.co.uk/blog/wipit/can-you-defame-the-dead> accessed: 10 May 2022
7. 'Can You Trademark a Voice?' (2022) <https://secureyourtrademark.com/can-you-trademark/trademark-a-voice/> accessed: 7 June 2022
8. 'Celebrity Rights in India' Legal Services India <http://www.legalserviceindia.com/article/l139-Celebrity-Rights.html> accessed 16 January 2022
9. 'Celebrity Rights: Protection under IP Laws' (2022) <https://docs.manupatra.in/newsline/articles/Upload/78DD5FE8-5C07-4075-934D-6917CD6BE868.pdf>

accessed: 24 January 2022

10. 'Defamation: Libel and Slander | ExpertLaw' (2022). <https://www.expertlaw.com/library/personal_injury/defamation.html> accessed: 8 May 2022
11. 'Defamation' (2022) <https://www.merriam-webster.com/dictionary/defamation> accessed: 8 May 2022
12. 'Diginoor to launch NFT of SP Balasubrahmanyam's unreleased song' (2022) <https://www.thehindubusinessline.com/news/diginoor-to-launch-nfts-of-sp-balasubrahmanyams-unreleased-song/article65267411.ece> accessed: 14 June 2022
13. 'Dilip Kumar, Saira Banu send defamation notice to builder' (2022) <https://indianexpress.com/article/entertainment/bollywood/dilip-kumar-saira-banu-defamation-notice-5523712/> accessed: 8 June 2022
14. 'Mail Today. Amitabh Bachchan to get copyright' (2022) available at: <https://www.indiatoday.in/movies/celebrities/story/amitabh-bachchan-to-get-copyright-85190-2010-11-08> accessed: 8 May 2022
15. 'The Hindu: Opinion / Leader Page Articles: Defamation litigation: a survivor's kit' (2022) <https://web.archive.org/web/20130722120816/http://www.hindu.com/2004/09/21/stories/2004092103551000.htm> accessed: 8 May 2022
16. 'Tort Law: The Rules of Defamation' (2022) available at: <https://lawshelf.com/shortvideoscontentview/tort-law-the-rules-of-defamation> accessed: 8 May 2022
17. 'Trademark' (2022) <https://www.law.cornell.edu/wex/trademark> accessed: 8 May 2022
18. 'Trademarks in United States of America (USA) - S.S Rana & Co' (2022) <https://ssrana.in/global-ip/

international-trademark-filing-registration/trademarks-in-united-states/> accessed: 8 May 2022

19. 'Wayback Machine' (2022) <https://web.archive.org/web/20140209044821/http://a4id.org/sites/default/files/user/Legal%20Guide_defamation.pdf> accessed: 8 May 2022)
20. 'When celebrities seek copyrights' (2022) <https://www.financialexpress.com/archive/when-celebrities-seek-copyrights/729569/> accessed: 7 May 2022

• • •

Printed by Libri Plureos GmbH in Hamburg,
Germany